The Step-by-Step Way to Draw Kawaii Wolfs

A Fun and Easy Drawing Book to Learn How to Draw

Kawaii Wolves

By

Kristen Diaz.

License Notes

No part of this Book can be reproduced in any form or by any means including print, electronic, scanning or photocopying unless prior permission is granted by the author.

All ideas, suggestions and guidelines mentioned here are written for informative purposes. While the author has taken every possible step to ensure accuracy, all readers are advised to follow information at their own risk. The author cannot be held responsible for personal and/or commercial damages in case of misinterpreting and misunderstanding any part of this Book

Table of Contents

Introduction

Becoming a great artist requires creativity, patience and practice. These habits can flourish in children when they start to develop them at a young age. We believe our guide will teach your child the discipline and patience required to not just learn to draw well, but to use those qualities in everything they do. Your job as a parent is to work with your child and encourage them when stuck and feel like giving up.

The world of art is an amazing way for you and your child to communicate and bond. When you open this book and start to create with your little one, you will delight in the things you learn about them and they will feel closer to you. Your support and gentle suggestions will help them be more patient with themselves and soon they will take the time needed to create spectacular drawings of which you can both be proud.

This guide is useful for parents as it teaches fundamentals of drawing and simple techniques. By following this book with your child, adults will learn patience and develop their skills as a child's most important teacher. By spending a few hours together you will develop a strong connection and learn the best ways of communicating with each other. It is truly a rewarding experience when you and your child create a masterpiece by working together!

How to draw a kawaii wolf!

Step 1.

Let's design a series of cute wolf cubs having fun! Start by drawing a circle for the head and add some ears on top. Add a small nose and an indication of where the snout will be. Then the outline of the body.

Step 2.

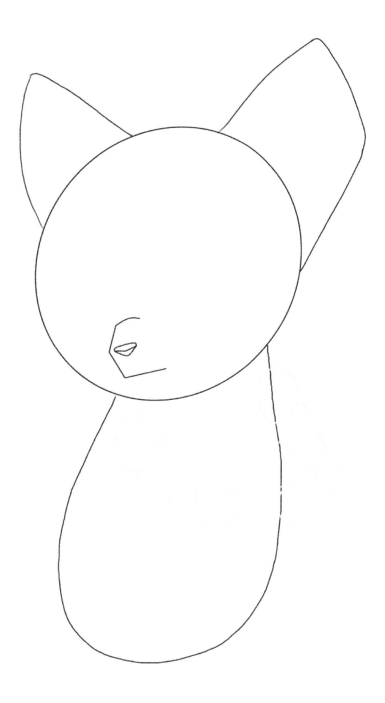

Add a circle for the shoulders and a circle for the elbows. Connect them to make the arm and add the paws.

Step 3.

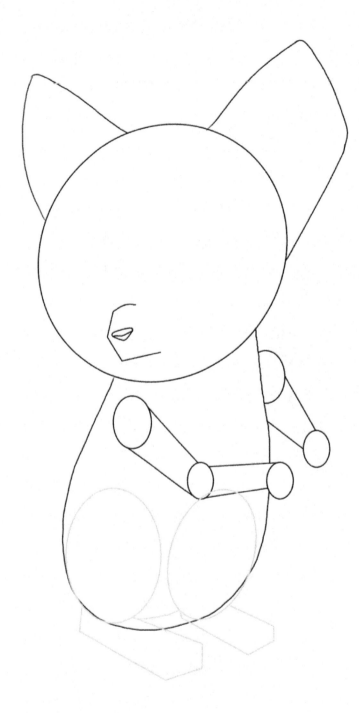

Now draw two ovals for the upper legs, and rectangles for the

lower leg.

Step 4.

Add a big smooth shape behind the cub for the tail.

Step 5.

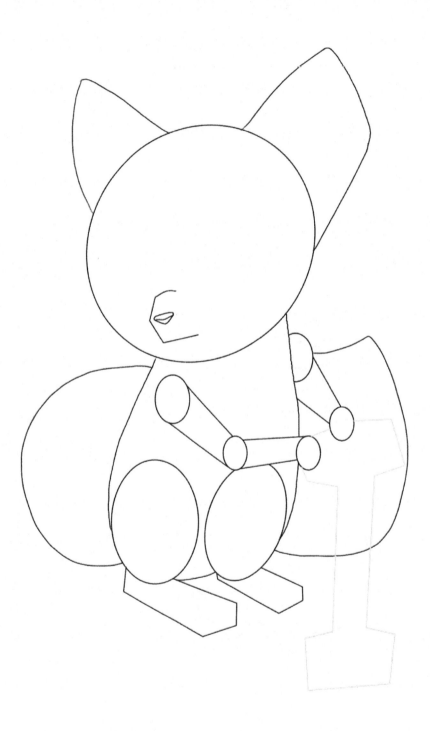

Let's give this cub a giant bone to play with! Add an outline of a

bone beneath its paws.

Step 6.

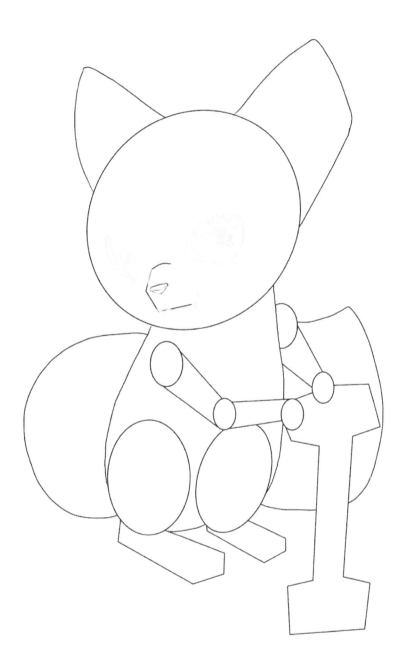

Draw two ovals for the eyes and add the pupil and iris inside.
Then redraw the snout to smooth it out and from the W shapes
upper jaw. Draw a fang on each side to make it even cuter.

Step 7.

Wolfs have lots of fur! Draw lots of spikes of fur around the cheeks, the ears and the top of the head. Make sure to add some plucks on top of the ears themselves.

Step 8.

Draw the mane on the chest of the cub. Make it full to make it seem fluffy. Then smooth out the arms resting on the giant bone.

Step 9.

Reshape the body to make it a little chunkier. Then add the belly fur and fur on the legs. Redraw the lower legs and give them some toes.

Step 10.

Add some cute eyelashes to the side of the eyes. Then reshape the
tail with loads of plucks to give it fluffy fur.

Step 11.

Redraw the bone to give it a smoother look. Then add more random plucks of hair across the body to add some detail.

Step 12.

Done! How does yours look? Let's color!

Step 13

Most wolves have a darker color for their fur. For this reason, I colored mine dark grey with light grey for the tips of the paws, legs, tail and ears. The eyes are a nice blue, to show how sweet this cub is. The bone is light yellow and the mane on her chest is also light grey.

Step 14.

Give her some shadow and highlights to make her come to life!

Step 15.

Colored version. She's sitting in a forest before the first snow falls.

Step 16.

Line art version.

How to draw a kawaii wolf!

Step 1.

Let's design a series of cute wolf cubs having fun! Start by drawing a circle for the head and add some ears on top. Add a small nose and an indication of where the snout will be. Make her snout open as if she's howling at something. Then the outline of the body curving behind the body itself, to give us a bird's eye perspective.

Step 2.

Add two rectangles for the paws pointing straight to the ground.

Step 3.

Now draw an oval for the upper leg, and a rectangle for the lower leg. The other leg is hidden behind her body.

Step 4.

Add a big smooth shape behind the cub for the tail.

Step 5.

Draw two ovals for the eyes and add the pupil and iris inside.
Then redraw the snout to smooth it out and from the W shapes
upper jaw. The lower jaw is opened and forms a smile, showing
that's she's excited for something. Maybe the snow is about to
fall? Add her teeth inside the jaw with a fang in each corner. Add
a tongue to complete it.

Step 6.

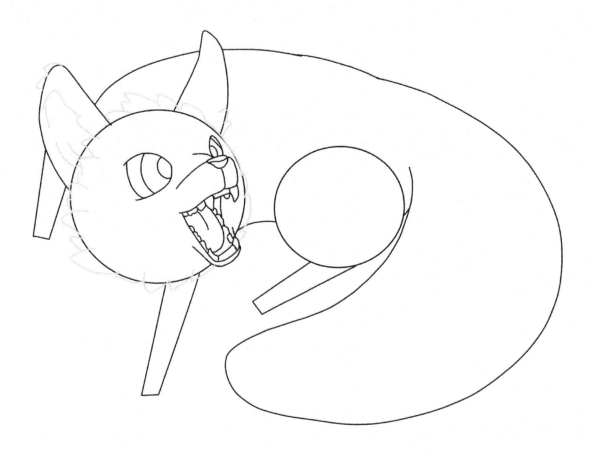

Wolfs have lots of fur! Draw lots of spikes of fur around the cheeks, the ears and the top of the head. Make sure to add some plucks on top of the ears themselves.

Step 7.

Draw the mane on the chest of the cub. Make it full to make it seem fluffy. Then smooth out the arms standing firmly on the ground.

Step 8.

Reshape the body to make it a little chunkier. Now add some fur on the legs. Redraw the lower legs and give them some toes.

Step 9.

Add some cute eyelashes to the side of the eyes. Then reshape the tail with loads of plucks to give it fluffy fur.

Step 10.

Add more random plucks of hair across the body to add some detail.

Step 11.

Done! How does yours look? Let's color!

Step 12.

Most wolves have a darker color for their fur. For this reason, I colored mine dark grey with light grey for the chest fur, the tips of the paws, legs, tail and ears. The eyes are a nice blue, to show how sweet this cub is. The tongue is pink with red for the inside of her mouth.

Step 13.

Give her some shadow and highlights to make her come to life!

Step 14.

Colored version. Look! The snow had fallen! Now we know why she's so happy!

Step 15.

Line art version.

How to draw a kawaii wolf!

Step 1.

Let's design a series of cute wolf cubs having fun! Start by drawing a circle for the head and add some ears on top. Add a small nose and an indication of where the snout will be. Then the outline of the body.

Step 2.

Add a circle for the shoulders and a circle for the elbows. Connect them to make the arm and add the paws. Have the paws curl up in front of her body, as if she's calm and relaxed.

Step 3.

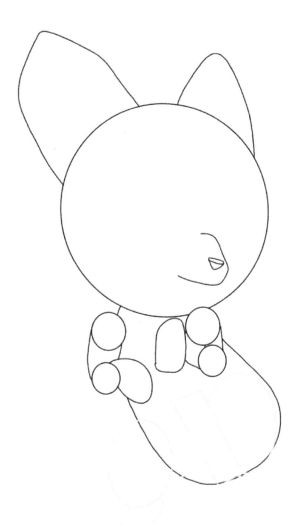

Now draw two ovals for the upper legs, and rectangles for the lower leg. Have one leg point upwards, while the other is pointing down, indicating that maybe she's lying down on something.

Step 4.

Add a big smooth shape behind the cub for the tail.

Step 5.

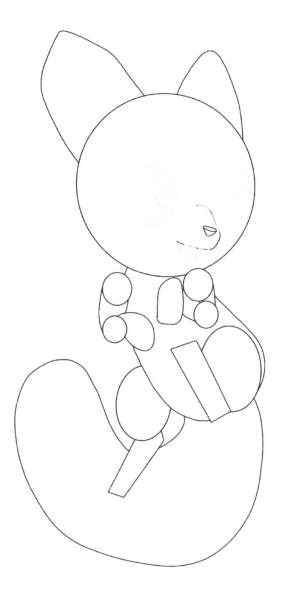

Draw two ovals for the eyes and add the pupil and iris inside.
Then redraw the snout to smooth it out and from the W shapes
upper jaw. Draw a fang on each side to make it even cuter. Add
the lower jaw opened up, showing that she's happy.

Step 6.

Wolves have lots of fur! Draw lots of spikes of fur around the cheeks, the ears and the top of the head. Make sure to add some plucks on top of the ears themselves.

Step 7.

Draw the mane on the chest of the cub. Make it full to make it
seem fluffy. Then redraw the paws and arms to make them
smoother.

Step 8.

Reshape the body to make it a little chunkier. Then add the belly fur and fur on the legs. Redraw the lower legs and give them some toes. On the leg pointing upwards, draw 4 cushions with her toes for her to walk on the ground without hurting herself. Then add a bigger cushion in the shape of a heart!

Add some cute eyelashes to the side of the eyes. Then reshape the tail with loads of plucks to give it fluffy fur.

Step 10.

Add more random plucks of hair across the body to add some detail.

Step 11.

Done! How does yours look? Let's color!

Step 12.

Most wolves have a darker color for their fur. For this reason, I colored mine dark grey with light grey for the main, the tips of the paws, legs, tail and ears. The eyes are a nice blue, to show how sweet this cub is. The cusions on her feet are dark red.

Step 13.

Give her some shadow and highlights to make her come to life!

Step 14.

Colored version. Look! She's rolling in the snow!

Step 15.

Line art version.

About the Author

Kristen Diaz is an accomplished artist and e-book author living in Southern California. She has provided the illustrations for hundreds of children's books as her realistic and lifelike images appeal to children and adults alike.

Diaz began her career as an artist when she was in her 20's creating caricatures on the beaches of sunny California. What started as a way to make extra spending money turned into a successful career because of her amazing talent. Her comically accurate caricatures had a unique look and one of the local authors took notice. When the writer asked Diaz to illustrate one of her books, Kristen jumped at the opportunity to showcase her talent. The result was spectacular and soon Diaz was in high demand. Her ability to change her style to fit the books made her an attractive artist to work with.

She decided to get a more formal education in graphic design and illustration by enrolling in the Arts program at Platt's College which is where she met the love of her life and life partner, Terri. The two live in Pasadena close to the beach where Diaz' career first flourished. She occasionally hangs out on the beach with her easel and paints and makes caricatures of the humanity passing by. Her e-books are simple to follow and contain many witty anecdotes about her life in Pasadena.

Made in the USA
Coppell, TX
30 April 2020

22361600R00031